# Hand it Over, Harry

## Don't Steal

Sarah Eason

**Enslow Elementary**
an imprint of
**Enslow Publishers, Inc.**
40 Industrial Road
Box 398
Berkeley Heights, NJ 07922
USA

http://www.enslow.com

It might be useful for parents or teachers to read our "How to use this book" guide on pages 28–29 before looking at Harry's dilemmas. The points for discussion on these pages are helpful to share with your child once you have read the book together.

Enslow Elementary, an imprint of Enslow Publishers, Inc.
Enslow Elementary is a registered trademark of Enslow Publishers, Inc.

This edition published by Enslow Publishers Inc.

**Library of Congress Cataloging-in-Publication Data:**

Eason, Sarah.
   Hand it over, Harry : don't steal / Sarah Eason.
      p. cm. — (You choose)
   Summary: "This title explores the story of one child who faces dilemmas about different social situations, the choices he or she makes and the consequences of those choices"—Provided by publisher.
   Includes index.
   ISBN 978-0-7660-4308-4
   1. Honesty—Juvenile literature.  I. Title.
   BF723.H7E27 2014
   179'.9—dc23
                                                   2012037707

Future edition:
Paperback ISBN: 978-1-4644-0561-7

Printed in China
122012 WKT, Shenzhen, Guangdong, China
10 9 8 7 6 5 4 3 2 1

First published in the UK in 2011 by Wayland
Copyright © Wayland 2011
Wayland
338 Euston Rd
London NW1 3BH

Produced for Wayland by Calcium
Design: Paul Myerscough
Editor for Wayland: Camilla Lloyd
Illustrations by Ailie Busby

Wayland is a division of Hachette Children's Books,
an Hachette UK company.
www.hachette.co.uk

# Contents

# Hello, Harry!

Harry is in a muddle. Like lots of children, he has new things to learn. He's finding that he can't always have everything he wants, and that being **honest** is sometimes hard.

Follow Harry as he finds himself in tricky situations in which he must choose to be **honest**.

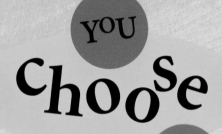

YOU choose too!

# Make Mom happy, Harry

It's Harry's mom's birthday tomorrow.

Harry wants to give her a present, but he doesn't have any money.

# What should Harry choose to do?

# Should Harry:

**a** take a bar of chocolate from a store without paying for it?

**b** pick some flowers from his neighbor's garden?

**C** make his mom a special card?

Harry, choose **C**

It's not the present that's important; it's showing Mom how much you love her. She would be really unhappy if she knew that you had taken something that wasn't yours.

What would YOU choose todo?

# Learn to share, Harry

Harry has been playing
at his friend's house.

His friend has the best digger EVER and Harry wants to take it home.

What should Harry choose to do?

**Should Harry:**

**a** break it so his friend can't play with it either?

**b** ask if he can borrow it for the weekend if he's really careful?

**c** hide the digger under his coat and take it home?

Harry, choose **b**

Being friends is all about sharing, not keeping things for yourself. You should ask before you borrow something. If you ask nicely, you will find that most people are happy to share with you.

What would YOU choose to do?

# Take it back, Harry

Harry is at the store and he's **bored**.

He cheers himself up by trying on sunglasses. When he leaves the store, he **realizes** that he's still wearing a pair.

# What should Harry choose to do?

**Should Harry:**

**a** put the sunglasses on his little brother?

**b** tell his mom and ask her to come back to the stor with him?

**c** take off the **price tag** and pretend they were always his?

Harry, choose **b**

It's much better to own up to a **mistake**. Grown-ups do understand. And it's okay to ask someone to stay with you if you're scared of owning up.

What would **YOU** **choose** to do?

# Be truthful, Harry

Harry is riding his bike at the park near his house.

A man walks past and drops some money by accident.

What should Harry choose to do?

## Should Harry:

**a** shout "Excuse me!" and tell the man he has dropped his money?

**b** put his wheel on the money to hide it and then pick it up when the man has gone?

**c** pick up the money and then pedal off really quickly?

Harry, choose **a**

You shouldn't keep things that aren't yours, even if you really want to. The man will think you are an extremely good boy for giving back his money, and you should feel very **proud**.

What would **YOU** choose to do?

# Earn it, Harry

Harry's Nana says
he can have a cookie.

As Harry reaches for the cookie jar, he sees a big pile of coins on the shelf. Harry doesn't have any money and wishes that he did.

What should Harry choose to do?

**Should Harry:**

**a** put two coins in his pocket – Nana won't notice that they're gone?

**b** take half of the coins and buy Nana a present?

**C** take a cookie and ask Nana if he can earn some pocket money while he's visiting?

Harry, choose **C**

Taking money without asking is **stealing**, even if you do plan to buy presents with it. But **earning** money makes you feel good, and Nanas usually love to find little jobs that you can do.

What would YOU Choose to do?

# Well done, Harry!

Hey, look at Harry! Now he has made honest choices, he's feeling much **happier**.

Did you choose the right thing to do each time? If you did, big cheers for you!

If you chose some of the other answers, try to think about Harry's choices to help you to be honest from now on. Then it will be big smiles all-round!

And remember – if it's not yours, hand it over!

# How to use this book

This book can be used by a grown-up and a child together. It is based on common situations in which any child might be tempted to be dishonest. Invite your child to talk about each of the choices. Ask questions such as "Why do you think Harry should give the money back to the man who dropped it?"

Discuss the wrong choices, as well as the right ones, with your child. Describe what is happening in the following pictures and talk about what the wrong and right choices might be.

- Taking things from other people is dishonest. Hand back something that isn't yours.

- Stealing from a shop is against the law. Don't do it! You will get into trouble, and your parents will, too.

- It isn't okay to steal something just so you can give it as a present. Think of other ways to make people happy.

Don't break things just because you can't have them. Ask to share and your friends might let you play with their toys, too.

Talk about the difference between right and wrong. Is there ever a time when taking might be the right thing to do? Help your child look for other options such as earning money, making a present, or simply showing how much he or she loves someone by trying to be good.

Try to explain that sometimes it is easier to be dishonest, but that stealing makes you feel bad about yourself. Making the right decision gives you a much happier feeling inside. Explain that it can also help you to feel better if you are honest about your emotions.

# Glossary

**borrow**—when someone lets you take or use something of his for a short time

**earning**—being given money for doing jobs

**honest**—telling the truth

**mistake**—getting something wrong

**muddle**—confusion or a mess

**price tag**—a label put on something in a shop to show how much you must pay for it

**proud**—feeling very pleased with yourself or with someone else

**realizes**—knows or understands

**sharing**—allowing others to use your things

**stealing**—taking something that does not belong to you

# Index

# Titles in the series

Library Ed. ISBN 978-0-7660-4306-0

Like all children, Carlos sometimes does things that are wrong, and doesn't come clean. He has lots of choices to make — but which are the TRUTHFUL ones?

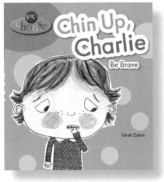

Library Ed. ISBN 978-0-7660-4305-3

Like all children, Charlie sometim feels a little sca He has lots of choices to make but which are th BRAVE ones?

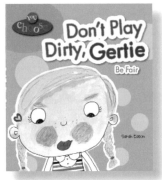

Library Ed. ISBN 978-0-7660-4307-7

Like all children, Gertie sometimes plays a little dirty. We put Gertie on the spot with some tricky problems and ask her to decide what is FAIR!

Library Ed. ISBN 978-0-7660-4308-4

Like all children, Harry sometime takes things tha don't belong to him. He has lots of choices to make — but whic are the HONEST ones?